WANTED!
FAMOUS OUTLAWS
JESSE JAMES

A NOTORIOUS BANK ROBBER OF THE WILD WEST

TIM COOKE

  Gareth Stevens
PUBLISHING

Please visit our website, **www.garethstevens.com**.
For a free color catalog of all our high-quality books,
call toll-free 1-800-542-2595 or fax 1-877-542-2596.

Library of Congress Cataloging-in-Publication Data

Cooke, Tim, 1961-
 Jesse James : a notorious bank robber of the wild west / Tim Cooke.
    pages cm. — (Wanted! Famous outlaws)
 Includes index.
ISBN 978-1-4824-4259-5 (pbk.)
ISBN 978-1-4824-4260-1 (6 pack)
ISBN 978-1-4824-4261-8 (library binding)
1. James, Jesse, 1847-1882—Juvenile literature. 2. Outlaws—West (U.S.)—Biography—Juvenile literature.
3. Frontier and pioneer life—West (U.S.)—Juvenile literature. 4. West (U.S.)—History—1860-1890—Juvenile literature.
I. Title.
F594.J27C66 2016
364.1552092—dc23
[B]
                              2015025044

Published in 2016 by
Gareth Stevens Publishing
111 East 14th Street, Suite 349
New York, NY 10003

© 2016 Brown Bear Books Ltd

For Brown Bear Books Ltd:
Editorial Director: Lindsey Lowe
Managing Editor: Tim Cooke
Children's Publisher: Anne O'Daly
Design Manager: Keith Davis
Designer: Melissa Roskell
Picture Manager: Sophie Mortimer

Picture Credits: Front Cover: Library of Congress. Alamy: AF Archive 42; Americasroof: 19, 32; Brown Bear Books: 6;
Elkman: 34; Ichabod: 20; Library of Congress: 4, 7, 10, 11, 13, 14, 15, 16, 17, 22, 24, 26, 27, 29, 31, 35, 39, 41, 43, 45; Papershke:
23; Robert Hunt Library: 8, 30; Shutterstock: Everett Historical 5, 12, 33, 36, 37, 38, 40, 44, Marzolino 28; Thinkstock:
istockphoto 25, Photos.com 9; Topfoto: The Granger Collection 18, 21.

Brown Bear Books has made every attempt to contact the copyright holders.
If anyone has any information please contact licensing@brownbearbooks.co.uk

Manufactured in the United States of America

CPSIA compliance information: Batch #CW16GS. For further information contact Gareth Stevens, New York, New York at 1-800-542-2595.

CONTENTS

INTRODUCTION

Jesse James was a bank robber, train robber, and murderer. He is famous as a feared outlaw of the Wild West. He loved **publicity**. He often wrote to newspapers about his crimes.

Jesse James even left press releases at the scenes of some of his robberies. They told journalists how to report the crimes. Jesse saw himself as a kind of hero. He wanted others to see him as a hero, too. Jesse believed that he was standing up for the right of the states to ignore the US government in Washington, D.C. Many people agreed with him.

Jesse James was born on September 5, 1847, in Clay County, Missouri. At the time, US settlement was

This photograph, showing five generations of a family of slaves, was taken in South Carolina.

spreading west across North America. In 1803, the United States bought a huge region west of the Mississippi from France. The deal was called the Louisiana Purchase. It included the area that became Missouri.

Political change

White settlers from the East Coast soon began to move into the new territory. They were looking for land to farm or the chance to set up a business, such as a store. In 1819, Missouri asked the US government if it could become a state.

The request caused a problem for the US government. The people in Missouri supported slavery. Like landowners in other Southern states, they wanted to use slaves to work on farms or **plantations**. However, people in northern states were against slavery.

Jesse James grew up in Missouri. He and his family believed people should be able to own slaves.

Publicity Attention paid to someone in the newspapers or other media.

Plantations Large estates for growing crops such as cotton, sugar, and rice.

If Missouri became a state, the slave states of the South would have more members in Congress than states that did not allow slavery. To keep the balance, Congress created the Missouri **Compromise** in 1820. This law separated Maine from Massachussetts to create a new "free" state. Missouri joined the **Union** as a slave state in 1821. Congress also ruled that new states that joined the Union north of a certain line would ban slavery. It seemed like the crisis had passed.

The Kansas-Nebraska Act

In 1854, the Kansas-Nebraska Act overturned the Missouri Compromise. The new law said that people living in the new states of Kansas and Nebraska could decide for themselves whether to be a slave state or a free state. In Kansas, many people opposed slavery, but many others supported it. The two sides clashed. There were violent fights.

The James family farm was home to Jesse, his brother Frank, and their sister Susan Lavenia.

Jesse James' family farm in Missouri lay close to the border with Kansas. The family followed stories about the growing violence in Kansas. They had a great effect on Jesse and his brother, Frank.

Compromise A solution to a dispute in which each side gives up some of its demands.

Union The United States of America.

A Frontier Upbringing

Jesse James grew up on the frontier. This was the very edge of the United States as white settlers moved westward across North America.

Jesse's parents moved to this farm in Missouri from Kentucky in 1842. His father grew hemp, which was used for making ropes.

Life on the Frontier was often hard. Families had to look after themselves. There were few towns or stores, or services such as plumbing. Many people were poor farmers. They worked hard to make a living. Many people in Missouri used slaves to help them work on their land.

Jesse's father, Robert James, was a farmer and a pastor at New Hope Baptist Church. He owned six slaves to help on his farm. In 1848, gold was discovered in California. Pastor James was one of the many people who rushed west to try to make a fortune. He arrived in California early in 1850. By the summer he was dead from **cholera**.

This photograph shows Frank (left) and Jesse James early in their career as outlaws.

Jesse's mother, Zerelda, remarried twice. Her second husband was a landowner, but he did not like Jesse or his brother, Frank. Zerelda's third husband was Dr. Reuben Samuel, whom she married in 1855. Later, he stopped practicing medicine to work on the family's hemp farm.

Supporting slavery

Like his father, Jesse believed people had the right to keep slaves. Jesse's neighbors shared similar ideas. Clay County was known for its support for slavery and the South. In 1854, men from Missouri crossed the border into Kansas. They voted illegally to allow slavery in the state. They did the same the following year. Now the opponents of slavery began to fight back.

ZERELDA JAMES

Zerelda (1825–1911) was a tough woman. She was known for having strong opinions. Zerelda supported the right to keep slaves. She always believed Frank and Jesse were heroes and defended their reputations. After Jesse's death in 1882, Zerelda sold souvenirs of her son to visitors to his grave, but she tricked them by selling fake souvenirs.

Cholera A disease that is usually caught by drinking infected water.

Focus: Bleeding Kansas

Kansas became a battleground between supporters and opponents of slavery. So much blood was spilled the state became known as "Bleeding Kansas."

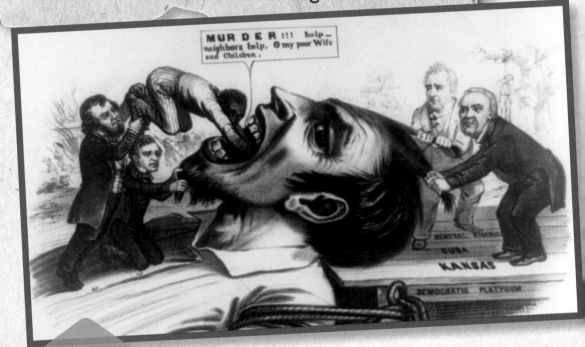

MURDER !!! help— neighbors help, O my poor Wife and Children.

CUBA

KANSAS

DEMOCRATIC PLATFORM

This political cartoon criticizes people who wanted slavery to be legal in Kansas. It shows a slave being pushed down the throat of an opponent of slavery.

In the summer of 1855, about 1,200 people from New England moved to Kansas. They wanted to make sure that Kansas became a free state. Southerners also headed to Kansas to try to make sure it became a slave state. Many came from Missouri. They were described as "border ruffians." They crossed the border to vote illegally in Kansas elections. They also carried out raids to scare people in Kansas into voting for a slave state. At one time, things became so confused that Kansas had two governments: one for slavery and one against slavery.

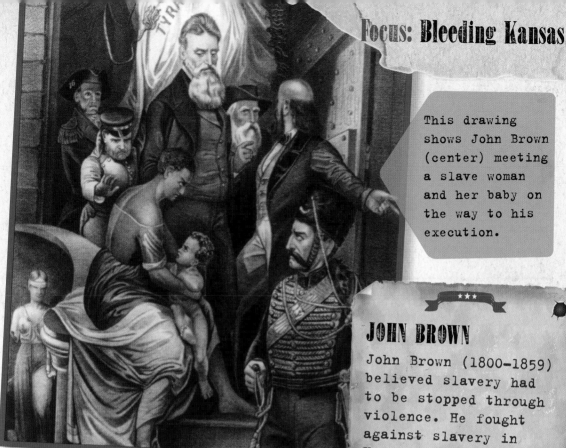

This drawing shows John Brown (center) meeting a slave woman and her baby on the way to his execution.

JOHN BROWN

John Brown (1800-1859) believed slavery had to be stopped through violence. He fought against slavery in Kansas. In 1859, he led a raid on the **federal** armory at Harper's Ferry, Virginia, to get more weapons. He hoped to start a slave rebellion. Brown was captured, tried, and hanged. He became a hero to the whole abolitionist movement.

John Brown

The most famous person to arrive in Kansas to fight against slavery was an **abolitionist** named John Brown. He led a small band of raiders who attacked pro-slavery settlers in Kansas for months. At Pottawatomie, Brown's band killed five men.

Frank and Jesse James heard about these clashes. Jesse was too young to join in, but Frank was older. He may have joined the border ruffians. But Jesse James was old enough to know what was going on—and which side he was on.

Abolitionist Someone who tried to make the government ban slavery throughout the country.

Federal Relating to the central government rather than to state or local government.

Focus: Bushwhackers

In 1861, the argument about slavery led to the outbreak of the Civil War. This set the Union, which opposed slavery, against the **Confederates,** who supported slavery.

Quantrill's Raiders fight against US Army soldiers they have trapped inside a house.

Alongside the regular armies, there were also groups of **guerrillas** on both sides. Both Frank and Jesse James joined bands of Confederate guerrillas known as "bushwhackers." Bushwhackers were groups of armed men. They mostly attacked families and farms in rural areas. They did not wear a uniform, but they saw themselves as a military force. Their opponents saw them as criminals who picked on those unable to defend themselves.

Jesse joins in

Frank joined Quantrill's Raiders. The band was greatly feared. It attacked Union soldiers and opponents of slavery on the Kansas–Missouri border. On August 21, 1863, Frank James and 450 others raided Lawrence, Kansas. They murdered 183 men and boys. When Jesse James was sixteen, he joined the guerrilla leader "Bloody" Bill Anderson and his group of bushwhackers.

Bushwhackers led by William C. Quantrill attack Lawrence, Kansas, on August 21, 1863. They chose the town because it was home to many opponents of slavery.

RAID ON CENTRALIA

Jesse James was among the bushwhackers led by "Bloody" Bill Anderson who carried out one of the worst atrocities of the Civil War. On September 27, 1864, Anderson's men rode into the small Missouri town of Centralia. They executed 22 Union soldiers. Witnesses called the massacre a "carnival of blood."

Guerrillas People who are not part of an army but who fight an enemy by using irregular tactics.

Confederates Supporters of the Southern side during the Civil War.

Postwar Missouri

The Civil War ended in Union victory in 1865. However, Missouri's problems continued after the war.

AN ORDINANCE ABOLISHING SLAVERY IN MISSOURI

The Emancipation Proclamation was issued by President Lincoln on January 1, 1863. It declared that all slaves in the Confederacy were now free.

In 1863 President Lincoln had freed all the slaves. The Republicans were in charge of Missouri. They began giving former slaves rights, such as the right to vote. This horrified former Confederates. The Republicans also punished those who had fought for the Southern states during the war. They took away their rights and brought in new laws. No one could vote unless they could prove they had not taken part in 86 different acts of rebellion during the Civil War.

The new laws left three-quarters of the white men in Jesse's home county unable to vote. Many people were unhappy. They resented the Union.

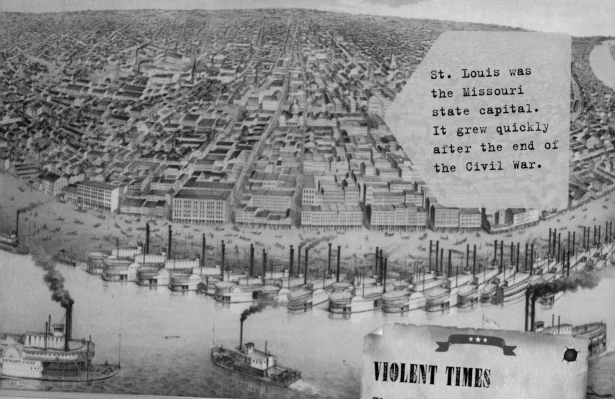

St. Louis was the Missouri state capital. It grew quickly after the end of the Civil War.

Fighting continues

Although the war had ended, fighting continued. The old arguments about slavery did not go away. The bushwhackers continued to raid their enemies. An election was due to be held in Missouri in 1866. To impose order during the election, Governor Thomas Fletcher sent state **militia** to fight the bushwhackers.

Meanwhile, Jesse James was starting to make himself known. He wrote a letter to a newspaper. He said that if one person robbed

VIOLENT TIMES

The fighting in Missouri was brutal. In some ways, it was like the fighting that had occurred between Native Americans and settlers a century before. Men fought each other hand to hand. Scalpings and stabbings were common, as were shootings. Missouri could be a very dangerous place.

Militia Citizen soldiers who are called on to fight in times of emergency or danger.

NATIONAL UNION
REPUBLICAN NOMINATION

FOR PRESIDENT.

Gen U.S. GRANT

...DENT.

...OLFAX

This poster supports the former Union general Ulysses S. Grant for president. He was elected in 1868.

JESSE'S ANGER

In 1872, the *Kansas City Times* newspaper printed a letter it said was from an anonymous outlaw. Most historians believe it was written by Jesse James. The letter said: "Just let a party of men commit a bold robbery, and the cry is hang them, but Grant and his party can steal millions, and it is all right."

another, he would be punished with death. But, Jesse wrote, President Ulysses S. Grant and the Republicans were stealing millions of dollars from the South. They were not being punished at all.

A disputed cause

In 1873 the Democrats took charge of Missouri from the Republicans. They set about reversing the laws that the Republicans had introduced. The Democrats believed that the Confederate cause during the Civil War had been a **noble** one. They argued that the South had been defeated in the war because the Union was powerful and wealthy. The cause itself was still worth fighting for. The Democrats opposed attempts at **Reconstruction**. They believed the North wanted to destroy the Southern way of life.

A criminal, or a hero?

Against this background, Jesse James decided that he did not have to obey the laws imposed by the government in Washington, DC. In fact, he believed that he had a moral right to attack any enemies of the Confederacy. They included businesses based in the North. He saw this not as becoming a criminal but becoming a hero. Jesse decided to turn to a life of crime. His brother Frank joined him. It was not long before they committed their first robbery.

Volunteers run a sewing class for freed slaves after the end of the Civil War. The Democrats did not want to give former slaves any civil rights.

Noble Having high personal qualities, such as fairness and loyalty.

Reconstruction The period from 1865 to 1877 when the government imposed conditions on the defeated Southern states after the end of the Civil War.

First Robberies

Jesse James most likely joined the bushwhacker leader, Archie Clement, to carry out his first robbery.

This photo shows Frank (left) and Jesse James with their mother, Zerelda.

On February 13, 1866, Archie Clement and his gang carried out a daring raid. They robbed the Clay County Savings Bank in Liberty, Missouri. It was the first ever daytime bank robbery in America. The raid set the tone for raids to come.

Daring raid

The Clay County Savings Bank was owned and run by Republicans, so it was a target for the bushwhackers. The raiders **pistol-whipped** the cashier. They stole as much as $58,000 ($753,000 in today's money) in bonds, paper money, gold, and silver coins. As they escaped, a passerby on the street was shot dead.

The Clay County Savings Bank still stands in Liberty, Missouri.

The raid seemed to have been carried out by bushwhackers, but the precise identity of the robbers has never been confirmed. Historians believe Jesse James was one of the bushwhackers. Eyewitnesses in Liberty later came forward. They identified both Frank and Jesse James as being among the members of the gang.

The **authorities** believed that Archie Clement was responsible. They hunted him down. Clement was finally shot dead by state militia in Lexington, Kentucky, on December 13, 1866.

LONG CAREER

Based on the length of his career, Jesse James was one of the most successful bank robbers in American history. It took fifteen years before he was captured. In that time, he put together a number of different gangs. But his robberies rarely went as planned. In many ways he was lucky to escape capture for as long as he did.

Pistol-whipped Hit someone with a gun, using it as if it were a club.

Authorities People who have the power to enforce laws.

Jesse Becomes Famous

Jesse grabbed the nation's attention when he shot dead a bank teller during a raid in Gallatin, Missouri.

The James Gang robbed their first bank in the small town of Gallatin, Missouri.

On December 7, 1869, Frank and Jesse robbed the Daviess County Savings Bank in Gallatin, Missouri. It is the first robbery where it is known for certain Frank and Jesse were involved. The cashier, John W. Sheets, was writing out a receipt for changing a $100 bill when Jesse shot him dead. Jesse grabbed a case of paper money as the brothers escaped. They left town chased by a **posse**. The money Jesse had grabbed was worth less than $1,000.

THE WRONG MAN

At Gallatin, Jesse thought he was shooting Samuel P. Cox. Cox was a member of the militia who had killed "Bloody" Bill Anderson. Anderson had been a member of Quantrill's Raiders. He also led his own gang. He killed many Union men in Kansas and Missouri during the Civil War. Anderson died when Cox shot him in a gunfight.

PROCLAMATION
OF THE
GOVERNOR OF MISSOURI!
REWARDS
FOR THE ARREST OF
Express and Train Robbers.

STATE OF MISSOURI,
EXECUTIVE DEPARTMENT.

WHEREAS, It has been made known to me, as the Governor of the State of Missouri, that certain parties, whose names are to me unknown, have confederated and banded themselves together for the purpose of committing robberies and other depredations within this State; and

WHEREAS, Said parties did, on or about the Eighth day of October, 1879, stop a train near Glendale, in the county of Jackson, in said State, and with force and violence, take, steal and carry away the money and other express matter being carried thereon; and

WHEREAS, On the fifteenth day of July, 1881, said parties and their confederates did stop a train upon the line of the Chicago, Rock Island and Pacific Railroad, near Winston, in the County of Daviess, in said State, and, with force and violence, take, steal, and carry away the money and other express matter being carried thereon; and, in perpetration of the robbery last aforesaid, the parties engaged therein did kill and murder one WILLIAM WESTFALL, the conductor of the train, together with one JOHN McCULLOCH, who was at the time in the employ of said company, then on said train; and

WHEREAS, FRANK JAMES and JESSE W. JAMES stand indicted in the Circuit Court of said Daviess County, for the murder of JOHN W. SHEETS, and the parties engaged in the robberies and murders aforesaid have fled from justice and have absconded and secreted themselves;

NOW, THEREFORE, in consideration of the premises, and in lieu of all other rewards heretofore offered for the arrest or conviction of the parties aforesaid, or either of them, by any person or corporation, I, THOMAS T. CRITTENDEN, Governor of the State of Missouri, do hereby offer a reward of five thousand dollars ($5,000.00) for the arrest and conviction of each person participating in either of the robberies or murders aforesaid, excepting the said FRANK JAMES and JESSE W. JAMES; and for the arrest and delivery of said

FRANK JAMES and JESSE W. JAMES,

and each or either of them, to the sheriff of said Daviess County, I hereby offer a reward of five thousand dollars, ($5,000.00,) and for the conviction of either of the parties last aforesaid of participation in either of the murders or robberies above mentioned, I hereby offer a further reward of five thousand dollars, ($5,000.00,).

IN TESTIMONY WHEREOF, I have hereunto set my hand and caused to be affixed the Great Seal of the State of Missouri. Done
[SEAL.] at the City of Jefferson on this 28th day of July, A. D. 1881.

THOS. T. CRITTENDEN.

By the Governor:
MICH'L K. McGRATH, Sec'y of State.

RUSH & FERGUSON, STATE PRINTERS, JEFFERSON CITY, MO.

Notoriety

It turned out that Jesse had killed Sheets because he thought Sheets was a man named Samuel P. Cox. Cox had killed Jesse's old bushwhacker commander, "Bloody" Bill Anderson. Like many of Jesse's robberies, things had not gone according to plan.

The Gallatin robbery was the first time Jesse's name had been definitely linked with a crime. The governor of Missouri offered a cash reward for the capture of Jesse and Frank. They were now officially outlaws.

As Frank and Jesse robbed more banks and trains, the rewards offered for their arrest increased.

Posse A group of citizens organized by a sheriff in order to enforce the law.

I Am Innocent

Jesse loved seeing his name in print. He rapidly became a household name thanks to a journalist for the *Kansas City Times*.

This photograph of Jesse with his gun helped to promote his outlaw image.

John Newman Edwards was editor of the *Kansas City Times*. He was a former officer in the Confederate Army. He wanted to get supporters of the Southern cause back into power. He thought Jesse James could help.

Robin Hood?

Six months after the Gallatin raid, Edwards published a letter from Jesse. Jesse argued that Union men were the real criminals, not the James brothers.

In 1873, Edwards used 20 pages of the *St. Louis Dispatch* to praise Jesse's exploits. He made Jesse seem like a modern-day Robin Hood. This English outlaw was said to have stood up for ordinary people against authority. Jesse was pleased with the

TOO LATE.

A Louisville Detective's Attempt to Discredit the Death of McDaniels.

Jesse James' Latest Expistolary Effort---A Poor Opinion of Bligh and Pinkerton.

The Louisville *Courier-Journal* still hugs Detective Bligh's delusion, that the dead bank robber was Jesse James. The identity of the dead man as Thompson McDaniels was first made known in the St. Louis *Times*, and the Associated press dispatches of yesterday confirmed the statement, on the very evidence which Detective Bligh forwarded to Kansas City. The following, from the *Courier-Journal*, was written before the news was received from Kansas City, and had it been delayed another day would probably not have appeared. With reference to the statement about the *Times* special, it need only be said that the *Times* correspondent did visit Pine Hill, saw McDaniels and fully identified him, After endeavoring to detect some inaccuracies in the *Times* special, the *Courier-Journal* says:

"The correspondent does not think that either the James or Younger brothers were in the Huntington bank robbery, and pretends that he recognized the dead man as Thompson, alias "Charley" McDaniels a noted desperado. The description of the men leaves no doubt that two of the Younger brothers were there, and possibly a third. While although the fourth might have been Jesse James, yet it was not McDaniels, as the description of the latter is entirely different from that of the dead man.

Thompson McDaniels is described as six feet high, sparely made, light or sandy complexion, light moustache, and thirty-two years of age. The dead robber was not over thirty, but rather younger, was dark complexioned, and had no light moustache.

Now comes the Nashville *American* with another letter from St. Louis, of which Jesse James is purported to be the author. The letter is sent as a special from Nashville, and is published below. It will be perceived that it is devoted to a denunciation of Captain Bligh and Detective Pinkerton, the two best detectives in the country. Captain Bligh is especially denounced in the severest terms in the letter. Coming as it does, from St. Louis, the authorship looks rather suspicious. The letter is entirely different in phraseology and spelling from any of Jesse James' former letters, the grammatical construction and spelling being generally good, although there is an attempt at a poor formation of sentences, while all of his former letters were illy constructed and very badly spelled.

[Special dispatch to the Courier-Journal.]

NASHVILLE, TENN., Sept. 24.—The following letter has been received by the

ST. LOUIS, Sept. 21, 1875.

To THE EDITOR OF THE AMERICAN:—In a previous communication I spoke of how the Jameses and Youngers had been lied on by Bligh, the incompetent detective of Louisville, Kentucky. I will take the present opportunity to inform you that Bligh's recent statement about the James and Younger boys, robbing the Huntington bank, is false. Instead of my being shot and captured, I am in St. Louis with my friends, well, feeling much better than I have for years. I can't see what motive any one can have in reporting such malicious lies as detective Blight is certainly doing. I know that Jarrett and the Youngers had no hand in the robbery, and if the wounded robber is ever recognized, it will undoubtedly be seen that he is not a James, a Younger, or Jarett. Bligh is a perfect gas-pipe, and is unworthy of the title of detective. He has never captured but one man and he slipped on the blind side of him. As for shooting, he doesn't know what that means. I am thankful that at least one robber has been got who was published everywhere by Bligh as being first Cole Younger and afterwards Jesse James. The world can now see that neither one of the Jameses and Youngers are the men shot and captured. Every bold robbery in the country is laid on us, but after a few of the robbers have been caught, and when it is seen two or three times that other people are robbing banks, bay be we will get fair play from the newspapers.

In a few days it will be seen how the Jameses and Youngers have been lied on by such men as Pinkerton and Bligh. I and Cole Younger are not

This newspaper report prints a letter from Jesse protesting that he is innocent of a recent robbery.

image Edwards created for him. Later he even named his own son after Edwards.

Jesse started to leave press releases at his crime scenes to ensure he received good publicity. He carried a copy of the Bible on his raids. That reinforced the idea that even though he was an outlaw he had right on his side.

ROBIN HOOD

Robin Hood was an legendary English outlaw in the Middle Ages, about 750 years ago. He led a band of outlaws who hid in Sherwood Forest in central England. Hood claimed that he only robbed the rich to help the poor. No one is certain that Robin Hood was a real person.

The James-Younger Gang

In 1868 the James gang joined forces with the Younger brothers to form the James-Younger gang.

This photograph shows Bob (left), Cole (front, center), and Jim Younger, with their sister.

The four Younger brothers were Cole, John, Jim, and Bob. They formed the core of the gang, with Frank and Jesse James. Other members joined at times. They included Clell Miller and other former Confederate bushwhackers. Jesse was the best known of the gang. Everyone thought he was the gang leader. In fact, the six main members shared power and made important decisions together.

Public support

The newspaperman John Newman Edwards continued to report news about the gang as if they were Confederate heroes. The gang continued to receive support from members of the public.

There were growing numbers of trains in the West. They became targets for gangs of robbers.

The two sets of brothers moved freely around their homes in Missouri. No one turned the gang into the authorities. In fact, the public helped to hide the gang. This made catching them very difficult.

In the early 1870s, the gang became more active. They robbed banks, stagecoaches, and even a fair in Kansas City. They also began robbing trains, in Missouri, Iowa, Louisiana, and Arkansas.

OFF THE RAILS

The gang robbed their first train on July 21, 1873. They derailed the Rock Island train in Adair, Iowa, and made off with $3,000. They often only robbed the guard's wagon, where valuables were kept. They usually left passengers alone.

His Reputation spreads

As the James and Younger brothers began raiding over a larger area, Jesse's fame grew.

Members of the Ku Klux Klan threaten the Republican politician George W. Washburn during a raid on his home.

The outlaws got more daring with their robberies. In June 1871 the James-Younger gang arrived in Corydon, Iowa. Most of the town was attending the local Methodist church. They were listening to a speaker named Henry Clay Dean. Dean was popular because he was an outspoken critic of the late President Abraham Lincoln. While everyone was inside the church, the gang robbed the Corydon State Bank of around $6,000 ($108,000 in today's money).

The Confederate general Nathan Bedford Forrest was a founder of the Ku Klux Klan.

Instead of running away, the James-Younger gang went to the church. They shouted out that they had robbed the bank. They also shouted "Catch us if you can." Then they left town.

The gang began to carry out raids as far south as Texas and as far east as West Virginia. In April 1872, they raided another bank in Columbia, Kentucky, and killed an unarmed cashier.

Bank robberies

The gang was growing more ambitious. They were not frightened of being arrested because there was little law and order in the West. It was a violent place. An organization called the Ku Klux Klan had emerged to resist the federal government. Many former Confederate soldiers were members. They attacked former slaves.

VIOLENT TIMES

The Ku Klux Klan was formed in the 1860s. Its members wore hoods to keep their identity secret. They harassed free slaves to stop them from voting for the Republicans. Members of the Klan beat or even killed African Americans in the South.

Focus: The Railroads

When the Civil War ended in 1865, more settlers headed west. Private companies built railroads that helped people travel to the West.

In the years leading up to the Civil War and after it ended, railroads were built across much of the country.

People in the South feared that the railroads would bring Northern laws and Northern settlers to their land. They saw the railroads as proof that the North was trying to control the whole country. Railroad building had started in 1828 with the construction of the Baltimore and Ohio Railroad. By 1860, every city in the North and Midwest was on a railroad. After the Civil War ended in 1865, the railroads headed west.

Railroad boom

For ordinary people, the railroads were a huge advance. Previously, long journeys were made by horse or stagecoach. Both were an uncomfortable way to travel. The new trains were **luxurious** in comparison. Trains did not only carry passengers. Goods such as grain, hogs, cattle, and money were also transported by train. It was the money that interested the James-Younger gang. They usually left any passengers alone.

This picture of a train yard shows passenger cars and boxcars used for carrying other cargo.

Luxurious Something that is very comfortable and often expensive.

Get Jesse!

As the gang carried out more raids, the railroad companies wanted to catch the outlaws. They turned to the famous Pinkerton detective agency.

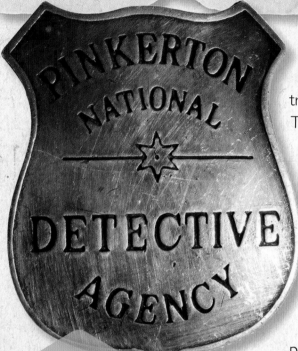

The Pinkerton National Detective Agency became the largest private security firm in the world.

On the afternoon of January 31, 1874, the Little Rock Express train was approaching Gads Hill. The town was 100 miles (160 km) south of St. Louis. It had a population of just 15. The James-Younger Gang was waiting there. They were all wearing Ku Klux Klan hoods. They had rounded up and robbed the town's residents. They stopped and robbed the train, including every one of the passengers. The gang got away with over $6,000 ($116,000 in today's money). The Adams Express Company owned the train. It wanted the outlaws caught.

The Pinkertons

Allan Pinkerton had founded a detective agency in 1850. The railroad hired it to catch the gang. The agency sent John W. Whicher to track Jesse down in March 1874. Whicher arrived in Clay County **undercover**. He asked about Jesse.

Allan Pinkerton (seated, right) and some of his men photographed during the Civil War.

The next day, Whicher was found shot dead. There was a note with the body. It threatened anyone asking about Jesse and Frank with the same fate.

Allan Pinkerton now took charge of catching the gang. His agents fought a gun battle with the Younger brothers. John Younger was fatally shot, as was an agent. Allan Pinkerton swore he would get even.

PRESS RELEASE

The gang handed printed notes to passengers at Gads Hill. It read: "The robbers were all large men, none of them under six feet tall. They were all masked. They were all mounted on fine blooded horses. There's ... excitement in this part of the country."

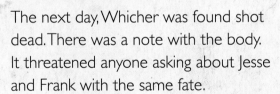

Undercover Taking on a different identity to gather information in a community.

Raid on the Homestead

Worse was to follow for the Pinkerton agency when a raid on the James family's farm went terribly wrong.

Today the James family farm is kept open as a historic site. Jesse is buried in the front yard.

Allan Pinkerton was outraged by the deaths of two of his agents. He decided to catch the James brothers at their home. He led a raid on the family farm on January 25, 1875.

A disaster!

Pinkerton agents and a posse from Clay County surrounded the farm. They threw a bomb made from a hollow iron ball filled with flammable jelly through a window. The bomb exploded in the fireplace. **Shrapnel** from the bomb killed Jesse's half-brother, Archie, and injured his mother, Zerelda.

She lost part of her right arm. Neither Frank nor Jesse was home so Pinkerton's agency had failed to catch them once again.

The bombing led to renewed support for the gang. Missouri politicians tried to pass a bill offering the brothers an **amnesty**. The bill was narrowly defeated. Meanwhile, the James brothers hunted down and killed any people who helped the Pinkerton agency.

This painting shows Jesse James fighting off the attackers. In reality, he was not even there.

I GIVE UP

The raid on the farm was the end of Allan Pinkerton's pursuit of Jesse James. He did not try to catch him again. Instead, the Pinkerton agency began working for coal and steel companies. The agents helped discover plans for strikes. They also used violence against striking workers.

Shrapnel Fragments of a bomb sprayed out by an explosion.

Amnesty A pardon for a crime.

The Final Raid

After the death of John Younger, Frank James wanted to retire. Jesse, however, wanted to carry on robbing banks in the South.

The First National Bank in Northfield was the target for the James-Younger gang's last raid.

In the summer of 1876, the gang decided to rob a bank in Minnesota. On September 7, 1876, the gang arrived in the town of Northfield, Minnesota. Their target was the First National Bank.

Poor planning

The gang split into three. Jesse, Frank, and Bob Younger were to rob the bank. Another group would act as lookout. The third group was to cover a getaway. The gang agreed that no civilians were to be shot. The raid went wrong from the start. No one inside the bank would open the **safe**. Outside, Northfield's storekeepers grew suspicious of the lookout team.

These guns used by Jesse and his gang were put on display in a museum in the 1920s.

Soon, the residents were involved in a shootout with the gang.

Escape!

All the gang members except Jesse were wounded or killed. Jesse and the wounded men fled, chased by the citizens of Northfield. For the next two weeks, the gang tried to get away to safety. Eventually, the James brothers split up from the others. They headed to Tennessee, where Jesse was living. That event marked the end of the James-Younger gang.

CITIZEN LAW

The people of Northfield succeeded where law agencies had failed. They ended the 15-year reign of Jesse and his gang. Many of the citizens were Civil War veterans. Some had fought the Sioux during clashes with the Native Americans in 1862. Many of them were also deer hunters. They all knew how to handle a gun.

Safe A strong fireproof box or room with a complex lock for storing valuables.

A New Gang

The raid at Northfield was the final
straw for Frank James. He retired.
Jesse kept his head down for a
while, but not for long.

Jesse and Frank
James settled in
small Western
towns where they
could remain
anonymous.

Both brothers moved to Tennessee. They lived
under false names. Frank called himself
B. J. Woods and Jesse used the name J. D. Howard.
Jesse tried to make a living by racing horses and
playing cards but he was a poor gambler. Soon
he was running out of money.

Another gang

Jesse also missed being in the public eye. In the
summer of 1879, he went back to Missouri to form
a new gang. His new gang carried out violent
robberies in Missouri and the South. But Jesse
no longer had the public's support. His long-time

champion, the newspaper editor John Newman Edwards, had also turned against him. He ignored Jesse's crimes.

By early 1882 Jesse was living in Missouri with his wife, Zee, and their two young children. He was putting together yet another gang. But he no longer trusted the members. He even murdered one of his own gang, Ed Miller. The only people he trusted were the brothers Robert and Charley Ford.

In this drawing from the time, the James-Younger gang rob people on a train.

Champion Someone who is a leading supporter of another person or a cause.

A New Recruit

Robert, or Bob, Ford was not even twenty-one years old when he shot Jesse James. James had no idea that the man he trusted would be his killer.

Bob Ford saw Jesse as a hero, but he later came to betray the man who trusted him.

Bob Ford was the youngest of seven children. His older brother, Charley, joined Jesse James's gang. He may have taken part in the Blue Cut train robbery of September 7, 1881. Growing up, Bob had admired what he heard about Jesse. He was eager to meet his hero.

Bob joins

Bob Ford met Jesse for the first time in 1880. At the time, Bob was nineteen. By 1881, the Ford brothers were living close to Jesse and his family in Missouri. Jesse soon came to feel that he could trust the Fords. When Jesse wanted to commit a new crime, he asked the Ford brothers to take part in a robbery in Platte City. The brothers turned down the offer. They had other plans.

A new governor

Thomas T. Crittenden had just been elected governor of Missouri. During the election campaign, he promised to bring the James brothers to **justice**. Bob Ford met with the governor on January 13, 1882. He got Crittenden to promise the Ford brothers a full pardon and a reward if they killed Jesse.

Crittenden had persuaded the railroad companies to offer a reward of $10,000 for each James brother, dead or alive. Frank had retired to West Virginia. Bob convinced Charley Ford that they had to kill Jesse. It was just a question of when.

By 1882, Jesse's latest gang had fallen apart. Dick Liddil, helped by Bob Ford, had shot Jesse's cousin. Jesse had killed Ed Miller for talking too much about their crimes. However, Jesse was still convinced that he could trust the Ford brothers. He even invited them to live with his family.

A NEW START

When Thomas T. Crittenden became governor, Missouri had a reputation in the rest of the country for lawlessness. He explained his intention to fight crime in his first speech. He said, "Missouri cannot be the home and abiding place of lawlessness of any character."

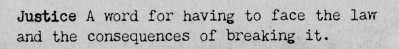

Justice A word for having to face the law and the consequences of breaking it.

Shot in the Back

Bob and Charley Ford did not have to wait long before they got their chance to make history.

GOD BLESS COOLA HOME

Bob Ford shoots Jesse. Shooting a man from behind was seen as the act of a coward.

Jesse James was always armed. He almost never took off his pistol. The Ford brothers knew they would lose any gunfight against him. They waited for a chance to catch him off guard.

On the morning of April 3, 1882, Jesse's wife, Zee, was cooking breakfast. Jesse was getting ready for a robbery. The Ford brothers were also in the house.

Fatal shot

As Jesse was going in and out of the house, he got warm and took off his coat. So that he would not draw attention to himself when he was outside, Jesse also took off his pistols. He then climbed onto a chair to dust a picture.

The Ford brothers drew their guns. Bob shot Jesse at **point blank** range in the back of the head. Jesse James was dead!

Claiming the reward

The Ford brothers gave themselves up at once. They were charged with murder but Governor Crittenden kept his word. He pardoned them. The brothers also received some of the reward money they had been promised, but not all of it.

This postcard appeared after Jesse's death. It shows key places in his life.

BOB FORD

After the murder, Bob Ford tried to make a career out of his new fame. He re-enacted the shooting and posed for photographs. But the public was outraged at the cowardly nature of Jesse's killing. Bob Ford had to flee Missouri for his own safety. He was later shot dead. Charley Ford took his own life.

THE HOUSE IN WHICH JESSE JAMES → → WAS KILLED.

THE HOME OF FRANK & JESSE JAMES

THE BAPTIST CHURCH KEARNEY MO. IN WHICH THE FUNERAL SERVICES WERE HELD.

Point blank When a bullet is fired very close to its target.

Focus: Jesse's Legacy

Jesse proved to be as popular in death as he had been for much of his life. People saw him as a romantic outlaw, not a cold-blooded killer.

In the movie *The Assassination of Jesse James by the Coward Robert Ford* (2007), Jesse was played by Brad Pitt (front, left)

Jesse James lived at a time when the West was opening up. People on the East Coast read cheap paperback books known as "dime novels." They loved reading about the daring things that happened in the West. Writers were quick to write exaggerated accounts of Jesse's exploits. Jesse became famous everywhere.

Jesse lives on

Jesse's family also cashed in on his fame. His mother, Zerelda, had him buried in her front yard. She sold pebbles from his grave to people who came to see the famous outlaw's final resting place. When they ran out, she sold them pebbles from her backyard.

Frank James gave himself up to Governor Crittenden five months after Jesse died. He briefly tried to cash in on his fame. He joined a touring show called the Buckskin Bill Wild West Show.

W.I. SWAIN'S WESTERN SPECTACULAR PRODUCTION

JESSE JAMES.

W.I. SWAIN

"THIS MONEY BELONGS TO ME"

This is a poster for a show based on Jesse's life that was popular during the 1880s.

He soon quit. Jesse's son, Jesse Jr., wrote a book entitled *Jesse James, My Father*. The only family member who did not cash in on Jesse's name was his wife, Zee. She refused an offer to write a book.

The first movie about Jesse James was made in 1908. Since then, Hollywood has been fascinated by the outlaw. Jesse has featured in countless films and stories as an example of a "noble bandit."

HERO OR NOT?

Some people saw Jesse as a symbol of the Southern cause. He saw himself in this way, as a romantic bandit. Other people saw him as an ordinary criminal and murderer. Jesse was certainly a pioneer: he was the first true bank robber. No one had robbed a bank before the James gang started.

ROGUES' GALLERY

Jesse was the most famous outlaw of his age. However, there were plenty of other outlaws who operated at the same time. Many rode with Jesse.

Belle Starr
(1848–1889)

Belle grew up with the James brothers in Missouri. She was known for her skill at shooting, and horse riding. Belle helped rustlers, bootleggers, and anyone outside of the law. She married a Cherokee man, Sam Starr (left). They settled down in Indian territory.

Archie Clement
(1846–1866)

"Little Arch" was a pro-Confederate guerrilla leader and bushwhacker. He was known for his violent attacks on Union soldiers. He and the James brothers carried out the 1866 bank raid in Liberty, Missouri. Clement died in a gun battle with state militia soon afterward.

"Bloody" Bill Anderson
(1840–1864)

William T. Anderson was a pro-Confederate guerrilla who rode with Quantrill's Raiders. After he fell out with Quantrill, Anderson formed his own gang, which Jesse James joined. In September 1864 Anderson's men captured a train in Centralia, Missouri. They killed 24 Union soldiers on board; later that day they ambushed and killed 100 more Union soldiers. A month later, a Union soldier named Samuel P. Cox shot Anderson dead in a gunfight.

Cole Younger
(1844–1916)

Thomas Coleman "Cole" Younger fought with Quantrill's Raiders during the Civil War. When peace returned, Cole and some of his brothers may have joined Archie Clement's gang. The first robbery in which Cole definitely took part was in 1868, when the Younger brothers—Cole, John, Jim, and Bob—first teamed up with the James brothers. In September 1876, Cole, Bob, and Jim Younger were captured after robbing a bank in Northfield, Missouri, and sentenced to prison for life. Cole was released in 1901, after serving nearly 25 years in prison.

GLOSSARY

Abolitionist Someone who tried to make slavery against the law.

Amnesty A pardon for a crime.

Authorities People who have the power to enforce laws.

Champion Someone who is a leading supporter of another person or a cause.

Cholera A fatal disease that is usually caught by drinking infected water.

Compromise A solution to a dispute in which each side makes concessions to the other.

Confederates Supporters of the Southern side during the Civil War.

Federal Relating to the central government rather than to state or local government.

Guerrillas People who fight an enemy by using tactics such as ambushes or assassination.

Justice A word for having to face the law and the consequences of breaking it.

Luxurious Something that is very comfortable and often expensive.

Militia Citizen soldiers who are called on to fight in times of emergency or danger.

Noble Having high personal qualities, such as fairness and loyalty.

Pistol-whipped Hit someone with a gun as if it were a club.

Plantations Large estates for growing crops such as cotton, sugar, and rice.

Point blank When a bullet is fired very close to its target.

Posse A group of citizens organized by a sheriff in order to enforce the law.

Publicity Attention paid to someone in the newspapers or other media.

Reconstruction The period from 1865 to 1877 when the government imposed conditions on the losing Southern states at the end of the Civil War.

Safe A strong fireproof box or room with a complex lock for storing valuables.

Shrapnel Fragments of a bomb sprayed out by an explosion.

Undercover Taking on a different identity to gather information in a community.

Union The United States of America.

FURTHER RESOURCES

Books

Burlingame, Jeff. *Jesse James: I Will Never Surrender*. Americans: The Spirit of a Nation. Berkeley Heights, NJ: Enslow Publishers, 2010.

Collins, Kathleen. *Jesse James: Western Bank Robber*. Famous People in American History. New York: Rosen Publishing Group, 2003.

Frish, Aaron. *Jesse James*. Legends of the West. Mankato, MN: Creative Education, 2005.

Green, Carl R., and William Sanford. *Jesse James*. Outlaws and Lawmen of the Wild West. Berkeley Hights, NJ: Enslow Publishers, Inc., 2008.

Robinson, J. Dennis. *Jesse James: Legendary Rebel and Outlaw*. Signature Lives. Minneapolis, MN: Compass Point Books, 2006.

Woog, Adam. *Jesse James*. Legends of the Wild West. New York: Chelsea House Publishers, 2010.

Websites

http://www.pbs.org/wgbh/americanexperience/features/introduction/james-introduction/
A site to support the program about Jesse James in the PBS *American Experience* series, with many pages of features about James and his life.

http://www.history.com/news/history-lists/7-things-you-might-not-know-about-jesse-james
A list of suprising facts about Jesse James from History.com.

http://www.legendsofamerica.com/we-jessejames.html
Page from Old West Legends that asks, "Jesse James – folklore hero or cold-blooded killer?"

http://www.historynet.com/jesse-james
A collection of facts about Jesse James from Historynet, with links to other articles.

Publisher's note to educators and parents: Our editors have carefully reviewed these websites to ensure that they are suitable for students. Many websites change frequently, however, and we cannot guarantee that a site's future contents will continue to meet our high standards of quality and educational value. Be advised that students should be closely supervised whenever they access the Internet.

INDEX